CONTENTS & CAUTION

Dear Dedicated Reader,

Sometimes it can be difficult to separate the WISE poems from the WITTY and WACKY ones! However, I trust in the viewing discretion of my WILD and WONDERFUL audience to be able to figure out what is what. Please keep in mind that these poems are for entertainment purposes ONLY and are not to be confused with actual view points of the author or his audience.

These poems do NOT revolve around any ONE particular topic but are incredibly RANDOM in nature and are simply there for your viewing pleasure and enjoyment. Surprisingly, many of them are about multiple guys named "Charley!"" If this happens to be your name than lucky you! Looks like your options in life could be quiet varied and exciting! Perhaps someone will write a poem about you someday! The following paragraph SHOULD be a legal disclaimer but is actually NOT.

The rereading of any single poem may cause an overwhelming need to share its content with others and may be accompanied by sudden outbursts of random rhyming! This brilliant and bizarre behavior may be temporarily tolerated but should be rapidly reported to the author immediately before such symptoms continue to persist and spread!

You may e-mail him at: JRCarlsonPoetry@Gmail.com. Thank you for your abundant support and he hopes to hear from you soon! (Alright, so perhaps "HE" refers to "HIMSELF" in third person on occasion but who doesn't right?)

Sincerest Regards,

J.R. Carlson

<u>*Outwitting Halfwits*</u>

I am a wise and witty man

Who used to be so full of plans.

It's hard to use my skill and charm

On people who are so unarmed.

I give and give and give some more

To mindless people who just ignore.

Their lack of care and understanding

Rocks me to the core.

A lesser man might start a fight

To justify wrongs and make them right.

We look to the future, that brighter day

When all will be made A.OKAY!

Some people really don't have a clue.

That's why outwitting halfwits is what I do!

The Watchmaker

I tell you a tale that's sad but true

About a watchmaker and his crew.

The workers had nothing to keep track of time.

Getting paid by the hour was just out of line.

If time stopped and everyone froze

The watchmaker's shop still wouldn't close.

There would be plenty of clocks left on the wall.

The big and small hands all having a ball

Round and round they'd continually go

Never stopping or getting slow.

The workers are mad and starting to shout!

"Hey man, where do we clock out?!"

A Whopping Fish Story

"It's time you knew the truth," said he.

I caught a 400 pound fish you see!

It was angry and rather hard to catch.

One might say a diabolical retch!

But that's just putting it simple and plain.

The truth is, it was really a pain.

It was like hunting for Big Foot and going insane!

By the way, I met Tarzan and Jane

After wrestling a lion and cutting off its main.

I didn't do it for fortune and fame.

I did it for YOU....

So you don't think I'm LAME!

Bob's Life Roller Coaster

There once was a man whose name is Bob.

He lost his wife, his car and his job.

Country music he played on the daily.

It truly annoyed his neighbor Baily.

It's also how he lost his wife Kaily.

Eventually Bob moved to a quaint little farm.

He chopped down a tree and it fell on his arm.

He went to the hospital to help him recover.

There he found his one true lover.

She happened to be his beautiful nurse

Who carried a gigantic sized purse.

Old Bob's doing really well now.

He owns a big farm and a whole lot of cows!

Bob got his life back.

He has a new wife and even a Cadillac!

Country music is still his thing.

His wife doesn't mind when he sings.

As long as she's out of the house

He won't lose his beautiful spouse!

McDoogle's Poodle

There once was a man named Fredrick McDoogle.

He was full of information.

Some called him Google.

He loved his wife and owned a nice car.

He never got drunk or went to a bar.

He owned a few mansions along the west coast.

That's why people loved him the most.

He was famous and rich

And never a snitch.

One day he bought a poodle

And only fed him noodles.

That pup didn't last very long

Especially after a couple of songs.

McDoogle tried to sing.

Only death he did bring.

His poodle died.

McDoogle cried.

That's the end of this story

In all of its fame and glory!

It was totally sad.

And really horribly bad!

Moving on before we all go mad!

<u>*Charley With a Harley*</u>

I once met a man with a super long beard.

It was long, black, scraggly and weird!

He had a deep voice and a big tattooed arm.

I could tell he didn't work on a piggy farm.

He lived to ride, and rode to live.

He was intelligent, witty, and would always give.

Some people were a little scared of him

Including this little kid named Tim.

Tim was tiny, small and lean

Basically the opposite of this giant machine!

Truth be told, this man was bold.

He was kind hearted, daring and nice.

He always gave the best advice.

He used to drive a Harley.

This man was my Uncle Charley.

My Friend Stew

Truth be told, I'm charming and bold.

Never too old for an adventure I'm told.

So I went out today to frolic and play.

I met an old man the old fashioned way.

I stuck out my hand to shake it a few.

He smiled and said, "My name is Stew."

I talked for a while and got back a smile.

It was time to leave or so I was told

By a police officer standing out in the cold.

Who would have guessed that Stew's life was a mess?

He was on the run while I was having fun.

They put Stew in a police car and took him down town

Just when I thought another friend had been found.

I guess this story just goes to show

That finding friends can go rather slow.

An Old Cashier's Life

This constant feeling of being too old

Is like a snow storm so freezing cold.

It's a feeling of terrible dread

That just might leave me buried and dead.

To the grave I continually go

Ha! Just kidding....

There's more to this show!

My boss would be so aggravated

If I showed up agitated.

A store cashier is not easily replaced.

There, I think I just made the ultimate case!

Besides, think of all the people I'll meet.

I wouldn't meet them living on the street.

This job is loads of fun

Especially when you're the owner's son.

One day this place could be mine!

Until then I'll take care of this line

And watch the clock, one day at a time!

Facebook Vice

Facebook is so great and nice.

It can be an addictive vice.

I messaged a cute girl once or twice.

She ignored me cause she has lice.

I might as well talk to mice

Or just eat some chicken and rice.

Friends should not come at such a high price.

This story doesn't really make sense

Which is exactly why I am so tense!

So next time someone messages you

Think twice about this little clue!

If I Were God

Lord thank you for thy gift of love.

I know it's sent from up above.

I try to share with others too

But I do not live where you do.

If I had limitless power to freely give,

A lot more people would definitely live!

More people would live healthy and strong

And love their lives that become extra-long.

Pain would leave incredibly quick

From those who are dying or terribly sick.

Suffering would be a thing of the past

And healing would begin at last!

Dream Girl

I met the girl of my dreams the other day.

She was wild, carefree and knew how to play.

She was witty and humorous with a smile from above.

But most of all she was kind, gentle and knew how to love.

On a more serious note, she knew how to cook bacon.

With this quality, I'm surprised she was not taken!

I can't help but greatly despise

All of the other guys that catch her eyes.

To impress her, I cooked up some fries.

They only added to my size.

The next cute girl I did meet

I found her jogging on the street!

She was skinny, thin and in great shape

Just like bacon on a plate!

The Thief Who Stole My Heart

Hickory dickory dock

Someone stole my clock!

A thief broke in

And now she's kin!

Hickory dickory dock

I caught the girl red handed.

She was a cute little bandit!

She was a charmer

And I disarmed her.

Hickory dickory dock

The time has flown by since then.

We have a few kids, okay maybe ten!

As far as the grandchildren know

Their grandparents met at the store.

Oh the joy of lying and not even trying!

Hickory dickory dock!

Give Me Some Credit

Give me some credit

And please pay your dues.

Think of the children

And their rotten hairdos.

Think of the clowns

And their silly little wigs.

Think of the ants and why they move twigs.

It's all the same

Having fortune and fame.

But not giving me credit

Is totally LAME!!

Living With Aliens

There is totally a place

To live in outer space

Where the aliens roam

And the clouds look like foam

To shoot phasers and call them lasers

To jump over craters and save others for later

Where time stands still and we stare at Bill

Where Bill stares back and we don't keep track

Until eventually we're hit with a smack!

Time we look the other way

Because staring is rude

Or so they say.

But that's what happens living in space.

Bill might smack you right in the face.

It's best to remember your rightful place.

He's not even human or part of your race.

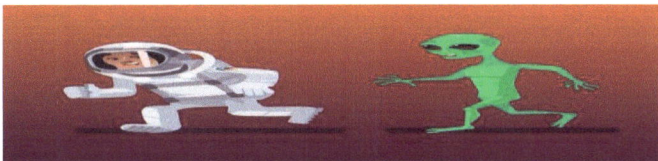

The Perfect Salesman

I once met a man traveling door to door.

He sold knives, watches, and items galore.

His pitch was amazing and hard to ignore.

One might say, "he was far from a bore!"

So I bought his wares and put them in store.

The number of items was far more than four!

Although, those purchases I did adore.

I never used them or thought of them more.

I ended up going on a World tour

And saw every ocean from shore to shore.

World travel is far from a chore.

While in Jamaica, I learned some folklore.

Salesmen can be pretty hardcore!

Keys to Success

If at first you don't succeed

Lose your pride and throw away your greed.

If by then you plant a seed

You will realize your lack of need.

You got bucked off that angry steed

And now it's time to take the lead.

Remember you have knowledge and power

That will manifest from hour to hour.

Courage and truth are your sword and shield.

There is protection on this playing field.

Someone loves you someone cares.

Your thoughts are in our daily prayers.

These are not just words on a page.

These thoughts will unlock your horrible cage!

A Golfer's Prayer

God in Heaven, please heal my body.

I know I'm not perfect and am a bit naughty!

Give me six-pack abs and arms made of steel

With a dazzling smile and looks that could kill.

I pray that I'm not asking for too much

But while you're at it

I'll take a tuna sandwich for lunch

And if you're still listening

My golf game probably makes you shutter.

So I could really use a solid gold putter!

No need to rush, I'll expect a delay

But of course, you're God! You could do this all

TODAY!

The Rat Race

I am a slave to my wants and needs.

The pain behind them drives my greed.

People say money doesn't grow on trees.

Then how will I ever become free?

I only have one life to live.

My precious time for dollars I give.

Work, eat and sleep some more.

It drives me crazy to the core!

Craziness, madness and life is a bore.

To end it all, I go to the store!

Endless Work

Work, work, I work all day.

There is no time to stop and play.

From sun up to sun down, I never quit.

Everything I do is incredibly legit!

Some people might stop to think

Why the heck I don't need a shrink!

Many people continually say

It's just a job that pays

And for a small fee

I would totally agree!

Education Motivation

If I had a dollar every time someone said

Why I'm at school and not in bed

I'd be flat broke and probably dead

Or writing with a pencil made of lead.

Homework is always such a drag

Every-time I put it in my bag.

I think to myself, what is the point

And then I see someone smoking a joint.

Homeless bums can be motivation

To get up and get an education!

Treasures of Truth

A diamond of truth is there for you.

It starts with a map and ends with a clue.

It goes from the beginning and straight to the end

Around a few trees and over a bend.

A big fat X you will find

When you finally come to the end of the line.

After digging through dirt for many long hours

You'll finally find the source of your power.

After much searching, the truth is told.

Finding yourself is better than gold!

<u>*Dating Advice*</u>

A picnic basket is so great

When you take someone on a date.

When you arrive, don't be late

Or you might not attract a mate.

Bringing food is important as well.

Wearing cologne will make you smell swell.

Attractive shoes are easy to spot

And body odor must never be caught.

In the end you will be glad

You listened to me and not your Dad.

It will bring you endless joy

No matter girl or boy.

Drinking and Driving

Drinking and driving is easy to do

Especially when everything is divided by TWO!

This is what happened to a girl named Sue.

Two red lights came into view.

Her senses were slowed as she slammed on the brakes

By then it was far too late!

She ran right into a girl named Kate!

They were both full of rage and had lots of hate.

A clean slate is what we all need.

Take heed to this tale if you want to thrive.

No one should EVER drink and drive!

Scoffers and Skeptics

Scoffers and skeptics are one and the same.

They critique, laugh and always place blame.

They always look for an error or a flaw

No matter how great something they saw.

Perhaps someday there will come a time

When they will perfect a craft so sublime

It will take more than power of wills.

It will take talent, hard work and skills.

When they have finally fulfilled their dream

A scoffer and skeptic will start to scream!

"What you made is not good enough!"

All the critiques will get kind of rough.

In the end they will finally see

Mocking and jeering isn't all it's cracked up to be.

The Super Cool Photographer

Taking pictures is easy

Especially when people are cheesy!

I don't need a staff to make others laugh.

Fake smiles are not my style

Even if your name is Kyle.

Genuine and unique is the way to go.

Keep it real and have a great show!

Let's be real for a second or two.

Having an untied shoe

Can be a problem for you.

You don't want that in the pic

Even if you are a homeless hick.

A hillbilly without any dough

Could never pay for a photo.

Come dressed nice and clean

And don't make a scene

Until I say so!

Drumming Obsession

I play the drums like a mad man.

I even bang on tin cans!

Wherever there's something to tap

I'd even slap someone's lap!

The rhythm just gets under my skin

I would even smack a shark's fin!

Okay, I may be obsessed.

I think it's time to invest

In some gloves and mittens.

I'd sound soft as a kitten.

The neighbors would not be annoyed

If I were suddenly deployed.

Into the army I'd go

To play my drums some more.

I'd join their band

And get a big hand.

Applause would finally come

When I play their giant bass drum!

Hooray for me!

People would see

A drummer I am to be!

Poetry for Cheerleaders

Rickity rackity rust

We're not allowed to cuss.

But nevertheless we must confess

That poetry is the best!

It gives us time to think

And makes us want to drink.

Lemonade and Gatorade

We never poor down the sink!

We always lose track of time

Shouting these catchy rhymes!

But nevertheless we must confess

That poetry is the best!

It's time for us to stop

Or maybe we will pop.

We're full of Razza Mu Tazz

And all of that jazz!

Poetry is the best!

The Woman Who Loved to Cook

There once was a woman who fried up some bacon.

She lost track of time and got it forsaken.

The smoke cleared and the alarm turned off.

All that woman could do was cough!

She didn't give up her cooking though.

She started making some heavy bread dough.

She added some water and then the flour.

It only took a good half an hour!

Eventually the mess was over and done.

Being a cook was a whole lot of fun.

She couldn't help but say this out loud.

Gosh, this woman was incredibly proud!

To be a great cook takes a whole lot of lovin'

Especially when fire comes straight from the oven!

The Small Town Clown

A tractor, a trailer, an old desert town

All of these things are quiet profound.

A place of silence and very little sound

A time when people could once be found

And giant ant hills are no longer around.

This is the home of Charley the Clown.

He once had a life of laughter and fun

Until his big head blocked out the sun!

It didn't rain for weeks on end.

The crops never grew again!

He lost his job and his friends moved away

Never to return to that town of Bombay.

Charley felt helpless and very much torn

And that is how this sad clown was born.

We now move on to a happier time

When Charley decides to become a mime.

He moves on to the town next door

Where the people think he is such a bore.

This clown is now down and out.

Although, he will never cry or pout.

He just switched jobs with his friend named Jack.

The company is called, "Planes with Cracks."

He flies bomber planes or so they say

And he's flying back to the town by Bombay!

GOOD Jokes for: FREE!

BETTER Jokes for: MONEY!

BEST Jokes for: NEW PLANE!

The Piper's Evil Son

Tom was once the Piper's son.

He lit a match and away he run.

The house went KABOOM!

His father was doomed!

The Piper was completely toast

Until Tom saw him as a ghost.

The haunting never ceased

Until Tom became deceased.

The Piper and Tom met in heaven

On the 4th of July around elven.

They gave each-other a hug

Along with all of their love.

Perhaps it was fate

For the long wait

Or perhaps it was a plan from above

For them to forgive and show love

But truth be told

Their hearts were cold

And neither one would ever tell

That they were trying to avoid Hell!

Rotten Uncle Billy

Words have meaning or so they say.

Rotten Uncle Billy would cuss every day.

His anger and temper were always so charged.

I think it stopped him from living so large.

He scared away his family and friends

Never caring if he saw them again.

He lived for himself and no one else

And that is why he lost his girl Chels.

He can't see the error of his ways

No matter how much we talk, even for days!

I've finally given up on this man

He has no hope or even a plan.

He's grumpy, rude and always so mean

If he died today, it wouldn't mean a thing.

Maybe one day he'll see his potential

And see that he could be influential

Or maybe God will set him straight

And not let him into the pearly gates.

Then he'll dwell with the demons below

And make friends with all the lawyers and crows.

Perhaps my Uncle has sealed his fate

But for YOU my friend, it's not too late!

The Gift of Time

Time is such a precious gift.

It can give us such a lift.

If we didn't have so many scars.

We could focus more on stars.

Not one day would ever be shattered.

We could live lives that truly mattered.

If money wasn't such an issue

We could use it for toilet tissue.

While we're at it, let's cure cancer

And name the antidote Reindeer Prancer!

Think of the World that we could achieve

With a lot more love and much less greed.

Always hope for a better day

Where the World is safe and the children can play

Where the air is clean and the crops are too

This, my friend, I leave to you!

When the birds chirp freely and the water is fresh

I'm sure you'll have much less stress.

Think for a moment of a freshly squeezed lime.

That, my friend, is the power of time!

Crazy Charley McFin

Once upon a time

A man lost his mind!

He started out crazy and then got lazy.

His name was Charley McFin.

He got married and had twins.

They were both trouble makers

And now they are Lakers.

He is so proud of them now

And so is Betsy his cow!

He talks to her all the time.

Some say he's way out of line!

His wife's maiden name is McDonald.

Her sons are Mitchell and Arnold.

Their cousin's names are as follows:

Billly, Teddy, Freddy and Sue

Then Jimmy, Hennery and Stew

And last but not least

The girl who's a beast

Alice, the girl to dread

Her siblings all want her dead!

But don't be alarmed

She's cute and unharmed.

She is always a charmer

And a wonderful farmer.

A girl who smiles a lot

She never steals and gets caught.

She loves her life

And will make a great wife.

Getting back to Charley McFin

He's plowing the fields again.

The plow broke down.

Alice isn't around.

Where that girl did go

No one seems to know.

She's not here today.

That girl ran away.

She found a wonderful lover.

Her dreams she did discover.

Her husband was kissed.

Her family won't be missed.

If only they treated her right

She wouldn't have left their sight!

Some blame Charley McFin.

Others blame his kin.

His neighbor blames Betsy the cow

Because Betsy talks to him now!

No one would have guessed

That Betsy was possessed!

Doc Jimbo says it's for real

Every time he sends Charley the bill.

Charley misses Alice a bunch!

Betsy says, "She's just out to lunch."

Doc Jimbo says, "Betsy is as crazy as a bat!"

But he should probably check on Tina the cat!

<u>Chucky the Gambler</u>

A gambler is one of a kind.

He bets everything and pays no mind.

Getting rich would bring plenty of pleasure

Just like finding a chest full of treasure!

Sadly, this story is not about gold

But it's entertaining, so let it unfold.

There was once a man whose name was Chucky.

He rolled the dice hoping to get lucky.

He won four games right in a row

Then lost his cabin and all of his crows.

Yes he got desperate and bet his crows

And almost bet his machine that mows!

Oh, the lawn mower you blatantly ask?

Yes, your wit is up to this task!

Chucky also lost his cat named Flin.

Chucky will never gamble again!

House Sitting With My Hounds

The snow falls on the ground.

It never makes a sound.

It falls all over my hounds.

They howl with a growl.

I throw them a towel.

They do nothing but scowl.

I decide to let them in.

They dry off and howl again.

They remind me of a child.

They are so meek and mild

And couldn't survive in the wild.

They tear up this house every day!

This is not mere child's play.

They make a gigantic mess!

I think they are possessed.

This house isn't even mine.

It belongs to Douglas McVine.

I think he will be mad

To see his house looking this bad!

It makes me rather sad.

It's time to switch my job

And give the hounds to Uncle Bob.

He'll take them off my hands

Along with the four broken fans

And two ripped chairs

And five chewed up bears.

Mr. McVine will need a carpet replacement

Along with a brand new basement!

Those hounds of mine are way out of line!

Uncle Bob will take them.

He won't mind!

Robots for Hire

Two scientists sat in a lab.

One was sad.

The other was mad.

A new creation they had.

It was a robot lad.

He was quiet and rad.

This machine could dance and sing

And play the piano a tad.

It could also talk and blab.

The scientists left to call a cab.

They left the robot in the lab.

It grabbed a knife and began to stab.

Chemicals got smashed all over the floor.

The lab isn't there anymore!

The lab caught on fire.

The scientists retired.

The local paper now reads:

"Robots for hire!"

Monopoly Cash

There's one last thing I'd like to say

Even though it's the end of the day.

I'm glad you did all of your chores.

You mowed the lawn and ironed your clothes.

You washed the dishes and fed the fishes.

You fixed the plows and milked the cows.

You harvested the figs and herded the pigs.

You took out the trash and cooked the hash.

Now it's time I go to my stash.

You will now get paid with Monopoly cash!

The Tired Poet

I'm tired of writing rhymes.

They do nothing but waste my time!

If I had a dollar for every line I wrote

I could probably buy a small paddle boat!

You'd be surprised how some people think.

Some are crazy and need a shrink

Or just someone who knows

How poetry flows.

"It's like water under a bridge," said he

Or "getting cake from the fridge for me."

I'm the master of these rhymes you see

But I do not write them all for free.

I have a family to feed indeed.

My poems are like little seeds

That grow into gigantic trees!

Their branches fly into the air.

People stop and blatantly stare.

This is why I care so much.

Time to go and eat some lunch!

Timeless Wisdom

Be wise my friend, it's easy to do.

Just be careful and tie your shoes.

Brush your teeth and comb your hair.

Trust others and always be fair.

Always speak kindly to one another.

Good heavens, I sound like your mother!

Being yourself is old fashioned I'm told.

Instead, be honest, brave and bold!

Your future will be fantastic and grand

If you follow this ultimate plan.

I will lead you down the path that rocks!

But just remember to change your socks.

This book began with me outwitting you.

Now look what you've learned from this wise guru!

www.ingramcontent.com/pod-product-compliance
Lightning Source LLC
Chambersburg PA
CBHW041802040426
42448CB00001B/15